EARLY ACTIVITY PHONICS

by Betty Pollard

World Teachers Press

Published with the permission of R.I.C. Publications Pty. Ltd.

Copyright © 1997 by Didax, Inc., Rowley, MA 01969. All rights reserved.

First published by R.I.C. Publications Pty. Ltd., Perth, Western Australia.

Limited reproduction permission: The publisher grants permission to individual teachers who have purchased this book to reproduce the blackline masters as needed for use with their own students. Reproduction for an entire school or school district or for commercial use is prohibited.

Printed in the United States of America.

Order Number 2-5033
ISBN 1-885111-46-0

A B C D E F 97 98 99 00

395 Main Street
Rowley, MA 01969

EARLY ACTIVITY PHONICS

Introduction

This book is a large selection of activities based on the phonetic sounds of the English language. It is intended that the activities be used as an integral part of early teaching programs and that you will use the worksheets and the ideas on each page to help to introduce, teach or consolidate the basic sounds, depending on the needs of your class or of individuals within the class.

The activities are consistent throughout the book to allow for ease of use, and aim to consolidate and extend the vocabulary of young children. The activities also allow for a variety of teaching strategies, including whole-class, group and individual activities.

Contents

Page	Vowel Sound	Page	Vowel Sound
6	**at** as in cat	34	**en**
7	**at**	35	**eg** as in beg
8	**at**	36	**eg**
9	**at**	37	**ed** as in bed
10	**am** as in jam	38	**ell** as in bell
11	**am**	39	**ell**
12	**ab** as in crab	40	**ot** as in hot
13	**ab**	41	**ot**
14	**ad** as in dad	42	**od** as in rod
15	**ag** as in bag	43	**op** as in top
16	**an** as in can	44	**op**
17	**an**	45	**og** as in dog
18	**ap** as in cap	46	**og**
19	**ap**	47	**ob** as in cob
20	**ip** as in dip	48	**ook** as in book
21	**in** as in bin	49	**ook**
22	**in**	50	**ub** as in tub
23	**im** as in dim	51	**ud** as in bud
24	**ib** as in bib	52	**ug** as in tug
25	**ib**	53	**ug**
26	**ig** as in pig	54	**up** as in cup
27	**ig**	55	**um** as in hum
28	**id** as in lid	56	**un** as in sun
29	**ill** as in hill	57	**un**
30	**ill**	58	**ut** as in hut
31	**et** as in net	59	**ut**
32	**et**	60	**ull** as in gull
33	**en** as in hen	61	**x** as in box

World Teachers Press — Early Activity Phonics

Teacher Information

Introduction

Activity Phonics is a series of blackline masters that focuses on introducing phonic sounds. As new sounds are introduced the activities in these books provide a specific focus on individual sounds. As students develop an understanding of the sound they are then able to complete more difficult activities that present the sound in context, imbedded in text.

The presentation and layout of each sound is deliberately similar. This ensures that the student is working on the sound being introduced and not absorbed in comprehending peripheral issues associated with page layout. It also allows for independent work by individuals who have experience working with this format.

Teachers can use the activities in this series in a variety of ways including:
- (i) whole class application when new sounds are being introduced.
- (ii) as revision of sounds.
- (iii) remedial work for students who are having difficulty with basic phonic sounds.
- (iv) extension work where the second activity in each pair is given to those students who demonstrate a good understanding.

Phonic Activities

In addition to the activities found in this series, the following activities can be used with each phonic sound to introduce, consolidate and extend knowledge.

- Construct booklets which display pictures with words containing the sound being treated.
- Sort selected pictures and words into sound groups.
- Locate words containing the sound within set passages or encourage students to locate the sound in their reading.
- Construct individual sound dictionaries with students.
- Ask students to create rhyming pairs for words with the same phonic sound.
- Use the phonic sound to build a word bank which can be displayed and added to as students discover new words with the same phonic sound.
- Display messages around the classroom which highlight the phonic sound being treated.
- Write letters to students which highlight particular phonic sounds.
- Sort words into common visual/sound pages.

Teacher Information - Example Lesson Development

Activity   'at' as in cat. Pages 6 and 7.

Introductory Work

Introducing new sounds to students is very important in the formation of early literacy skills. Students will have used most sounds in oral communication and now need to relate this oral usage to the written form. Therefore introductory activities need to start in the oral form working on the foundation that already exists. Ask students to provide their own examples of words with the specific sound, use pictures which show words with the sound in use.

With the oral work it is vital that the correct pronounciation is used. Misconceptions developed at the early stage will be very difficult to alter later on. Repetition of the sound and words containing the sound will assist in this area.

Completing the Worksheets

Each sound is supported by an activity sheet(s), that identifies words containing the sound and applies the words in simple language activities.

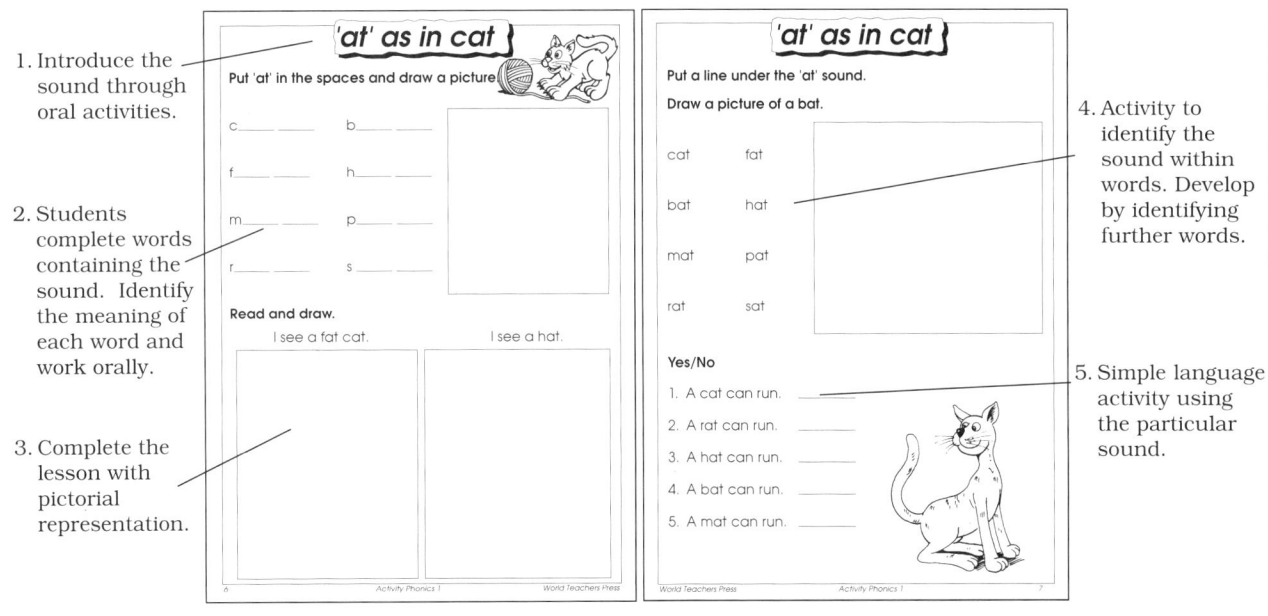

1. Introduce the sound through oral activities.

2. Students complete words containing the sound. Identify the meaning of each word and work orally.

3. Complete the lesson with pictorial representation.

4. Activity to identify the sound within words. Develop by identifying further words.

5. Simple language activity using the particular sound.

Extension

Extension activities should focus on identifying more words containing the particular sound and then using the words in practical activities such as writing short sentences and 'read and draw'.

'at' as in cat

Put 'at' in the spaces and draw a picture.

c___ ___   b___ ___

f___ ___   h___ ___

m___ ___   p___ ___

r___ ___   s___ ___

Read and draw.

I see a fat cat.   I see a hat.

'at' as in cat

Put a line under the 'at' sound.

Draw a picture of a bat.

cat   fat

bat   hat

mat   pat

rat   sat

Yes/No

1. A cat can run. _____
2. A rat can run. _____
3. A hat can run. _____
4. A bat can run. _____
5. A mat can run. _____

'at' as in cat

Read the stories.

My cat is fat.

My cat is black.

My cat is on the mat.

My cat has a hat.

I like my cat.

Draw the cat.

'at' as in cat

Put 'at' words on the cat.

His name is Nat.   He is a fat cat.

___at   ___at

___at   ___at

___at   ___at

___at   ___at

'am' as in jam

Put 'am' in the spaces.

Draw a picture.

h __ __   j __ __

P __ __   r __ __

S __ __   d __ __

Yes/No

1. Do you like jam? _____

2. Do you like ham? _____

Read and draw.

Sam and Pam sat by the dam.

'am' as in jam

Put 'am' in the spaces.

Strawberry Jam

d _____ _____

h _____ _____

P _____ _____

S _____ _____

r _____ _____

1. I like bread and _____ _____ _____.

2. _____ _____ is a boy.

3. _____ _____ is a girl.

4. A father sheep is a _____ _____ _____.

'ab' as in crab

Put 'ab' in the spaces.

Draw pictures for two of the words.

c____ ____   j____ ____

l____ ____   t____ ____

cr____ ____

Add 's'

crab____   tab____

Read and draw.

A man can see the crab.

The crab ran and ran.

'ab' as in cab

Put in the missing words.

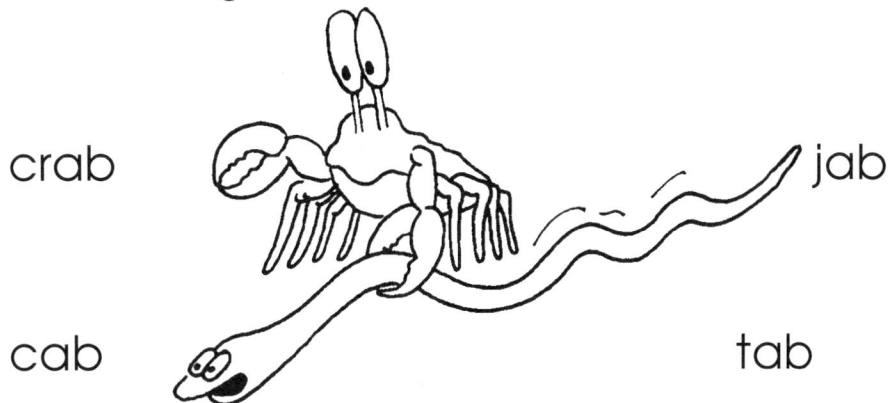

crab   jab

cab   tab

1. The _____ caught a snake.

2. I went in a _____.

Draw a crab.

'ad' as in dad

Put 'ad' in the spaces.

d_____   b_____

f_____   h_____

l_____   m_____

p_____   s_____

Put in the missing words.

sad   mad   pad

bad   dad   had

1. He is _____.

2. She is _____.

3. My dad _____ a van.

'ag' as in bag

Put 'ag' in the spaces.

b____ ____   l____ ____

r____ ____   s____ ____

t____ ____   w____ ____

Read and draw.

Sam has a bag.

My dog can wag its tail.

'an' as in can

Put 'an' in the spaces.

c_____ _____

D_____ _____

N_____ _____

r_____ _____

m_____ _____

f_____ _____

p_____ _____

v_____ _____

Read and draw.

A man is in a van.

Dan has a can.

'an' as in can

Yes/No

1. Mom has a pan. _____

2. Do you have a pan? _____

3. Do you have a fan? _____

Put in the missing word.

| ran | fan | man |
| pan | nan | can |

The man _____ to the van.

Read and draw.

Draw a van.

Color it blue.

'ap' as in cap

Put 'ap' in the spaces.

c_____ _____   g_____ _____

l_____ _____   m_____ _____

n_____ _____   r_____ _____

s_____ _____   t_____ _____

z_____ _____

Put in the missing words.

cap   tap   lap

gap   map   nap

1. Dad has a _____.

2. Baby will have a _____.

3. Can you read the _____?

'ap' as in cap

Put the 'ap' words on the cap.

Read and draw.

A cat can lap.

The man in the van has a map.

World Teachers Press — Early Activity Phonics

'ip' as in dip

Put 'ip' in the spaces.

d___ ___

l___ ___

s___ ___

t___ ___

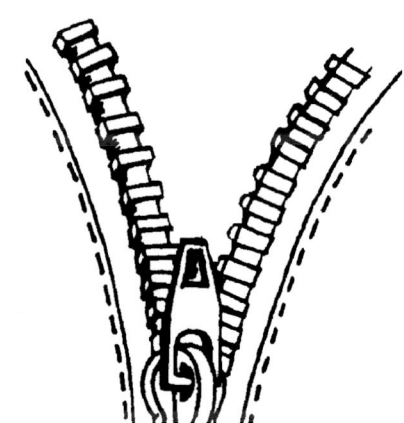

h___ ___

n___ ___

r___ ___

z___ ___

Yes/No

1. Can a truck tip? _____

2. Can you zip your coat? _____

3. Can you take a sip? _____

4. Do you have a hip? _____

5. Can paper rip? _____

6. Do you have a lip? _____

'in' as in bin

Put 'in' in the spaces.

b_____ _____   f_____ _____

p_____ _____   d_____ _____

sh_____ _____   w_____ _____

Yes/No

1. Can you see a bin? _____

2. Can you see a pin? _____

3. Do you make a din? _____

4. A fish has a fin. _____

5. Do you like to win? _____

6. Can you scratch your shin? _____

'in' as in bin

Read and draw.

A big bin and a little bin.

A cat is by the big bin.

A rat is by the little bin.

The rat sees the cat.

'im' as in dim

Put 'im' in the spaces.

d_____ _____

h_____ _____

r_____ _____

T_____ _____

sw_____ _____

Read and draw.

Tim can swim at the beach.

'ib' as in bib

Put 'ib' in the spaces.

b_____ _____

f_____ _____

cr_____ _____

r_____ _____

Read and draw.

Draw a bib. Put the words on the bib.

'ib' as in bib

Put in the missing word.

bib   crib   rib   ribs

1. Baby has a _____.

2. We have _____.

Yes/No

1. Do you have a bib? _____

2. Baby has a bib. _____

3. Do you have a rib? _____

Read and draw.

A baby has a bib.

'ig' as in pig

Put 'ig' in the spaces.

b_____   d_____

f_____   j_____

p_____   w_____

Put the 'ig' words on the pig.

'ig' as in pig

Yes/No

1. Do you like pigs? _____

2. Can you do a jig? _____

3. A pig has a wig. _____

4. Can a pig jig? _____

Read and draw.

There is a big pig and six little pigs.

A pig has a wig.

'id' as in lid

Put 'id' in the spaces.

d____ ____   h____ ____

k____ ____   l____ ____

r____ ____

Read and draw.

Little Billy Goat Gruff is a kid.

The kid hid behind the bin.

'ill' as in hill

Put 'ill' in the spaces.

h_ _ _   b_ _ _

f_ _ _   k_ _ _

m_ _ _   p_ _ _

s_ _ _   t_ _ _

w_ _ _

Put the words on the hill.

Draw Jack and Jill going up the hill.

'ill' as in hill

Put in the missing words.

Jill	hill	mill
bill	fill	kill
pill	sill	till

1. Jack and _____ went up the hill.

2. A duck has a _____.

3. The Little Red Hen went to the _____.

Draw a windmill.

'et' as in net

Put 'et' in the spaces.

Draw a picture.

n____ ____   j____ ____

b____ ____   g____ ____

l____ ____   w____ ____

s____ ____   m____ ____

p____ ____

Read and draw.

It is a wet day.

There is a pet in a jet.

'et' as in net

Put 'et' words in the raindrops.

'en' as in hen

Put 'en' in the spaces.

Draw pictures for two of the words.

h____ ____   d____ ____

B____ ____   p____ ____

t____ ____   m____ ____

h____ ____

Read and draw.

Ten men are by a jet.

'en' as in hen

Read and draw.

See the big fat hen.

The hen has ten eggs.

Yes/No

1. Ben is a girl's name. _____

2. A fox has a den. _____

3. We have ten legs. _____

4. We write with a pen. _____

5. A hen lays eggs. _____

'eg' as in beg

Put 'eg' in the spaces.

b_____ _____   k_____ _____

l_____ _____   p_____ _____

Add 's' to the words.

beg_____   leg_____

peg_____   keg_____

Draw a pair of legs.

'eg' as in beg

Put in the missing words.

leg   peg   beg   keg

legs   pegs   kegs

1. A dog can _____.
2. A dog has four _____.
3. I have two _____.

Read and draw.

A dog can beg.

I have two legs.

'ed' as in bed

Put 'ed' in the spaces.

b____ ____   f____ ____

l____ ____   r____ ____

T____ ____   w____ ____

Read and draw.

Draw a bed.

Put big Ted in the bed.

Color the bed red.

'ell' as in bell

Put 'ell' in the spaces.

Draw a picture for two of the words.

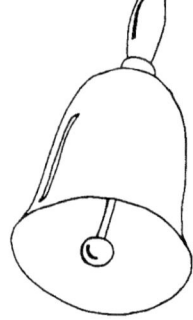

b_____ _____ _____   f_____ _____ _____

s_____ _____ _____   sm_____ _____ _____

t_____ _____ _____   w_____ _____ _____

y_____ _____ _____

Read and draw.

Put a bell on a well.

'ell' as in bell

Put in the missing words.

bell   sell   smell

yell   fell

tell   well

1. Jack and Jill went to the _____.

2. Do not _____.

3. We can _____ flowers.

4. Jack _____ down.

5. We will _____ a story.

6. We can ring the _____.

7. Can I _____ my old toys?

'ot' as in hot

Put 'ot' in the spaces.

Draw pictures for three of the words.

h_____ _____   c_____ _____

d_____ _____   g_____ _____

j_____ _____   l_____ _____

n_____ _____   p_____ _____

r_____ _____

Yes/No

1. Can a pot hop? _____

2. Is it hot today? _____

3. The sun is hot today. _____

4. Can you make a dot? _____

5. Do you sleep on a cot? _____

'ot' as in hot

Put the 'ot' words on the pot.

Read and draw.

Draw a boy on a cot.

Draw a hot pot.

'od' as in rod

Put 'od' in the spaces.
Draw two of the pictures.

c____ ____   n____ ____

p____ ____   r____ ____

Yes/No

1. A cod is a fish. _____

2. We catch fish with a rod. _____

3. Can you nod your head? _____

4. Peas are in a pod. _____

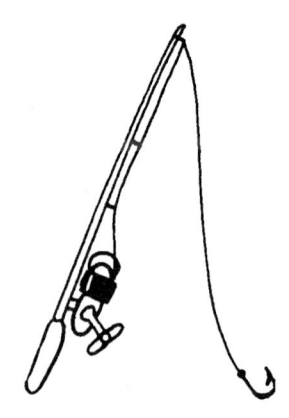

Read and draw.

There is a fishing rod and a cod fish.

'op' as in top

Put 'op' in the spaces.
Draw a picture.

h____ ____

m____ ____

t____ ____

st____ ____

Put in the missing words.

hop   top   mop   pop   stop

1. A car can _____.

2. I can _____ on one foot.

3. A _____ can spin.

4. Popcorn goes _____.

'op' as in top

Yes/No

1. Can you hop? _____

2. Popcorn goes pop. _____

3. Can you mop the floor? _____

5. Can a car stop? _____

Read and draw.

A colored spinning top.

'og' as in dog

Put 'og' in the spaces.

Draw pictures of some
of the words.

d____ ____   b____ ____

f____ ____   h____ ____

j____ ____   c____ ____

l____ ____   fr____ ____

Read and draw.

A frog is on a log.   A dog is by the log.

'og' as in dog

Put in the missing words.

jog   bog   dog   log

cog   fog   hog   frog

1. A _____ can jump.

2. It is fun to _____.

3. My pet is a _____.

4. A _____ is the same as a pig.

Yes/No

1. Can you jog? _____

2. Do you like hogs? _____

3. A frog can hop. _____

4. A dog can jog. _____

'ob' as in cob

Put 'ob' in the spaces.

B____ ____   c____ ____

j____ ____   m____ ____

s____ ____   r____ ____

                    b____ ____

Add 's' to the words.

sob____   cob____   job____

Read and draw.

There is a cob of corn. Color it yellow.

'ook' as in book

Put 'ook' in the spaces.

b ___ ___ ___

h ___ ___ ___

t ___ ___ ___

c ___ ___ ___

l ___ ___ ___

Read and draw.

There is a hook on the end of the fishing line.

There is a hat that a cook would wear.

'ook' as in book

Yes/No

1. Can you read a book? _____
2. Can you bait a hook? _____
3. Can you cook a meal? _____
4. Can you take a look? _____

Add 's'

cook_____   book_____   look_____

Read and draw.

Six books on a shelf.

'ub' as in tub

Put 'ub' in the spaces.

Draw pictures for two of the words.

c_____ ____

h_____ ____

r_____ ____

t_____ ____

Read and draw.

A cub is in a cave.

'ud' as in bud

Put 'ud' in the spaces.

Draw some of the pictures.

b___ ___

c___ ___

b___ ___s

d___ ___

s___ ___s

m___ ___

Read and draw.

Suds are in a tub.   There are ten pretty buds.

'ug' as in tug

Put 'ug' in the spaces.

Draw some of the pictures.

t_____ ____

b_____ ____

h_____ ____

j_____ ____

m_____ ____

r_____ ____

Yes/No

1. A tug is a strong boat. _____

2. We drink from a mug. _____

'ug' as in tug

Read and draw.

A tugboat is by a ship.

There is a blue jug.

Here is a red and yellow bug.

'up' as in cup

Put 'up' in the spaces.

Draw pictures.

c__ __

p__ __

c__ __s

p__ __s

Read and draw.

Seven cups. Color five blue and two yellow.

There are ten pups in a box.

'um' as in hum

Put 'um' in the spaces.

Draw a picture.

h___ ___

g___ ___

s___ ___

m___ ___

dr___ ___

Yes/No

1. I like sums. _____

2. A drum is fun. _____

3. Can you hum? _____

4. A mum is a flower. _____

5. Can you do this sum? 1+1= ☐ _____

'un' as in sun

Put 'un' in the spaces.

Draw some pictures.

s_____ _____

b_____ _____

f_____ _____

g_____ _____

n_____ _____

r_____ _____

Read and draw.

It is fun to run.

The sun is hot.

'un' as in sun

Put the 'un' words on the sun.

Yes/No

1. The sun is hot. _____

2. You eat a bun. _____

3. Can you run? _____

World Teachers Press   Early Activity Phonics

'ut' as in hut

Put 'ut' in the spaces.
Draw three of the pictures.

h___ ___   c___ ___

b___ ___   n___ ___

r___ ___

Yes/No

1. Do you like nuts? _____

2. Scissors can cut. _____

3. Do you live in a hut? _____

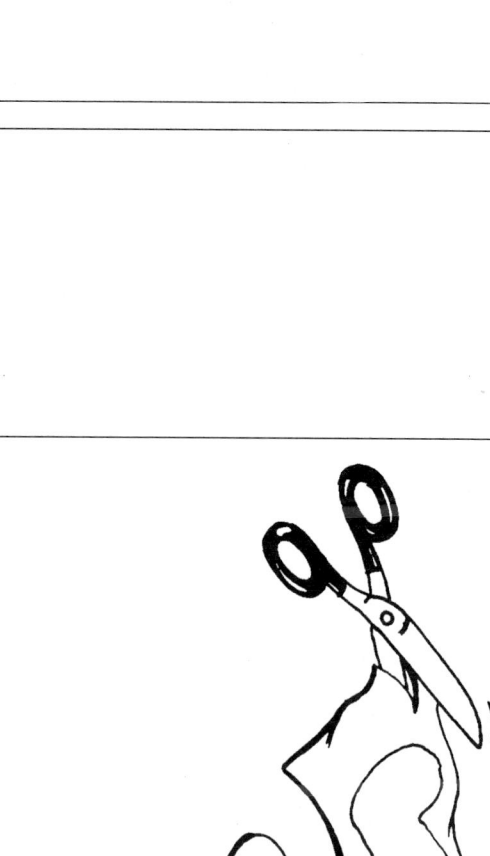

Add 's' to the words.

nut____   hut____   cut____

'ut' as in hut

Read and draw.

There are nine nuts in a bag.

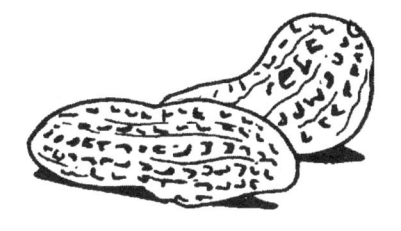

A hut is by a tree.

I can cut.

'ull' as in gull

Put 'ull' in the spaces.
Draw pictures.

d__ __ __

h__ __ __

g__ __ __

Yes/No

1. The sky is dull. _____

2. A gull is a bird. _____

3. A boat has a hull. _____

Read and draw.

Seagulls are flying in the sky.

'x' as in box

Put 'x' in the spaces.

Draw two of the pictures.

wa____ Ma____

si____ fi____

mi____ bo____

fo____

Read and draw.

A fox is on a box.

Max is six.

Early Activity Phonics

About the Author

Betty Pollard, Bunbury, Western Australia.
Betty has many years of teaching experience and specializes in the elementary grades. Her titles focus on the phonics area of language development and present a very structured, easy-to-follow approach. The success of her phonics books throughout the world has been outstanding and reflects the need in classrooms for materials that are developmental in nature and structured in format.